WAVES
OF
EMOTION

WAVES
OF
EMOTION

ARDEN H.

ARCHWAY
PUBLISHING

Archway Publishing books may be ordered
through booksellers or by contacting:

Archway Publishing
1663 Liberty Drive
Bloomington, IN 47403
www.archwaypublishing.com
844-669-3957

Because of the dynamic nature of the Internet, any web
addresses or links contained in this book may have changed
since publication and may no longer be valid. The views
expressed in this work are solely those of the author and do
not necessarily reflect the views of the publisher, and the
publisher hereby disclaims any responsibility for them.

Any people depicted in stock imagery provided by Getty Images are
models, and such images are being used for illustrative purposes only.
Certain stock imagery © Getty Images.

ISBN: 978-1-4808-9689-5 (sc)
ISBN: 978-1-4808-9690-1 (e)

Library of Congress Control Number: 2020918825

Print information available on the last page.

Archway Publishing rev. date: 11/02/2020

CONTENTS

I
TIDAL

—An exceptionally large ocean wave
caused by an underwater earthquake

—An overwhelming manifestation of
an emotion or a phenomenon

Lilac skies of broken hearts,
'Cause the lines don't always meet;
Then someone departs.
Tell me how all the heat
Began burning in this hallway.
While I left
You went your own way.
Letters of Post-it notes,
Sincere thoughts, and comforting warmth,
Yet the lies come forth.
Once again left in the dark,
My heart is sold.
These tears have told.
The fire burns out, and these words don't come out.
These words don't come out.

Clouds of discord
Running away from the shore.
The rain just poured.
It was us—I could've sworn.
Shapeless shadows walking in the night,
Tossing and turning into hopeless
Dreams.
Woken by a light.
Is this where she redeems?
Sunday's citizens walking the street,
Gradually done with being discreet.
No one knows her whole,
Tainted talk.
Liquid courage is not a friend,
Falling as they mock.
Just let the waves bend,
Tears of regret, cries of delight,
Head on the floor.
Everything wanted in plain sight.
Clouds of discord,
Pieces of broken,
Mirrored glass in the dust.
Sweetness is spoken.
Doesn't feel like lust.

We lay it out there,
Born into this,
Not a category
Or something to be.
But these thoughts echo loud enough.
We trot them to paper,
Suddenly scattered to pieces of letters.
To some they don't make sense.
To us every chamber of our heart
Tied together
By a slipknot.
Once we feel tugs
Everything tenses,
Clenched fists,
Slow breathing,
Stone-cold eyes and—

She looks
As if I am full of lies,
Realizing how I am pulling so hard
Against my own will
To show affection.
It's as if
I am strung to a puppeteer.
That releases all fear.
She holds me so tightly.
I become a flesh-covered stone.
Nobody's home.
Ringing in my ears
Screeches to let her in.

To let go

Effortlessly.

In words you found yourself the most,
A way of communication.
We have never understood
How effortlessly we could antagonize each other.
The peak of your voice
While every nerve inside is screaming to get out,
The walls shattering before you,
The mountains blanking out all
sight of any possible fear.
We dance to death from inside out,
As thorns of roses will pierce our skin, no doubt.
No wounds could take these words or thoughts,
Could take the truth of your high-pitched voice
Piercing every vein clutched to our hearts.

It fell.
She ran her fingers through her hair.
It's falling.
She stares with vulnerable, liquid eyes.
It's shattering.
She takes a step back.
It's everywhere.
What has awoken me
From nightmares,
Dried my tears
Despite the created fears?
Raises her voice.
There goes any choice.
She engulfs me.
Nowhere else I would rather be.

Feels so right.
When the waves come back
Everything else blurs. It is now
A craving to forget.
The tide pulls it all back to the day
Everything capsized,
Crashed as a tsunami.
Eyes looked
Vulnerable, closed, calm.
Your palm grazed softly
Against my neck
Then held tightly.

When my eyes closed finally,
Dropped my heart from my sleeve
Slowly.
All at once
Air escaped my lungs,
The thirst
In love.
Everything becomes rough,
The waves,
Rocky shore,
A want for more.
Through the day and night
To call you mine, would
Feel so right.
Stay my anchor.
We are a beautiful sight.

In a future life
Everything would
Feel so right.

II
INTERNAL

—Gravity waves that oscillate

—*Oscillation* is defined as "repetitive variation, typically in time of some measure about a central value or between two or more different states. Also occurs in dynamic systems" (Wikipedia).

—Example: the beating of a human heart

Let yourself lose it all,
Fall and break.
Let the shattered pieces
Continue digging in at every attempt to be together.
Trudge through the worst weather.
Find the tide that cleanses your whole soul
From outside to in.
Take your time to begin.
They said I am living in sin.
As it all trickled down,
The cleanse began.

Love is not just a word.
It changes us,
Makes us see so dim
Because they are the light of our life.

A kiss we never left,
A touch we forgot we kept,
A whisper we crave more,
A jolt we want an excuse,
A grip we will not let go,
Blissfully irresistible
Hands on shoulders,
Glides hands to hips,
Crashing through boulders,
Tides of full dips.
Heart shreds—it is tearing,
Fully rips.

Lighting matches,
Erasing all the sewn patches.
The fact I can get it right,
Already choking on my pride.
With you it is ride or die.
The fact I lost all self-esteem,
What does all this mean?
It is never as it seems.
She screams, and the rest
Is left in the sheets.
Flame ignited,
Burning everything, I confined in
Those vulnerable eyes that caged in
All ounces of purity,
Raged into morality,
Elbows dug into the mattress.
This fire.
Who lit the matches?
Gripping necks,
Two shipwrecks.
Blame it on the kerosene.
Vulnerable eyes, what had they seen?
A soul engulfed,
A bed life indulged.
Now the red life fades to dust.
We charcoaled in the lust.

The art of you stays in my mind.
How exquisite your taste in scripture
from white to black?
To gray all the way to black and blue,
Made of succulent skin.
Why do these bruises adore you?
Fond of tragedy,
Calm as tea
While you hold me tight.
In the far off now
Where is the then?
In these dreams
What year is it?
Bowed to one knee
While gazing into your eyes,
Your gasp to tears
The second time.
Your no-longer-vulnerable liquid eyes,
That crisp smile
Igniting fireworks
Through our hearts.
Aches clashing
To the first kiss.
We learned
Our love
Could never
Be allowed.

III
SHALLOW

—Water near the shoreline

—There's something near the surface.

—Not capable of serious thought

Tacenda.
What to live by?
Some may find dry.
A sign of fear,
A tendency of running
Away from any type of peer,
No matter where.
Over here,
Right there,
Nowhere near.
Escaped at the scraped-up stream,
Drowned at the perilous dream,
Choking down losing the very last beam,
Engulfed to brightness,
Blinded by righteousness,
Thoughts of peace,
A soliloquy of an endless dream,
Afloat with comfort and willfulness
That not everything is what it seems.

Everyone just gazed in awe.
Remember when giving up was simple?
Just a quick toss of the towel
Without a wonder of the difference
If kept going.
No, not anymore.
The rain it pours, but the sullen trudge it continues.
Drip drop, tick tock, a new day to get up.
Fake it until you make it.
The money is coming, but what is a dollar
When you can't even call her "mine?"
Time is never on your side,
Or this force of nature pulls apart
Any seams to be sewn.
It is becoming okay to be alone,
To depend on your own heart and soul.

Playing God,
Sitting at the bottom of the ocean,
Counting each grain of sand,
Why even plan?
I am sitting on the cold, hard ground,
Listening to every step, every sound.
I am sitting in a vibrant cloud,
Flicking every speck of water
To the ground.
I am sitting above
The glacier of Mars,
Thinking dreadful thoughts of stars.
Why even count stars?

Another day, another bottle.
Everything has become hollow.
A shattered hourglass
Trying to give the time of day.
Brains aching because of all the bottles drunk,
Every ounce for
A poisoned soul.
Words can no longer be pronounced,
Emptied instead of whole.

I loved her.
I cherished her.
I thought there wouldn't ever be another her.
This isn't a never-say-never type of thing.
It's that I still go back and have that same giggle
I did in our past while it was happening.
Type of thing.
It's that I don't have nightmares anymore.
I have dreams that she's still here.
Here,
While here I thought I was crazy,
When people talk of love I think of you.
When people ask me about my first time
I wish it had been you because you deserved that.
You deserved the innocent, vulnerable heart.
Then I think back, and you got it.
You rearranged my happy new well-being.
I built up, did my best to create just for you.
At the time it wasn't for anybody but me.
That's what made it pure again.

Struggles of love and anger.

I could never repay her

For holding me down

When there was no one to be found,

Risking it all when I am trying not to be found.

One day she will wake, taken back
to all the nights of us.
One day she will kiss and open her
eyes longing for it to be us.
One day she will cascade through
all our memories in her head.
I am not waiting for those days.
One day she will think of us at the exact
time I am troublesome sleep.
One day she will hear our song as
I am battling to breathe.
One day she will wash away every
inch of how close our skin was.
I am not waiting for those days.
No matter how we couldn't ever get close
enough, funny how that works.
I am not waiting for those days.
One day she will be sleepless. Her
thoughtless heart will come around.
One day she will be sleeping sound in
the arms that couldn't let go.
One day she will know that only in
dreams could they appear.
I am not waiting for those days.

"Will that be all today?"
"Yes, just this six pack of beer."

IV
REFRACTED

—Change of direction of waves that
occurs when they travel

—Refraction is a measurement of the focusing
characteristics of an eye or eyes.

My autumn sky.
Life couldn't ever feel so high.
Floating in the depths of your eyes.
Didn't ever think I'd get trapped in your lies,
A ghost figure.
I just, I'd do anything for her,
Trapped in this lure.
As her eyes rise with the tides
I've become blind,
Thinking I'm trapped in a bind
To choose,
But you've guided me this far.
I wonder if I'm up to par.
Surrounded by empty bottles,
Popping pills, binging for cheap thrills.
Seems I walked into the wrong bar,
Jumped off the edge,
Didn't grab hold.
In the moment,
Bold.
Can't get me, can't get me
On my knees.
Hold me up.
It's not an empty cup.
This dear-universe mentality,
It's hers, not my fatality.

I never thought I would get trapped in her lies.
It has been months.
I suppose she was not my forever autumn sky.
The seasons have changed,
Better days
Back in another autumn.
This time alone.
This time I am whole.

They unraveled every inch
Of her gorgeous skin,
Sharpening every thorn,
Only for my skin
To be pierced
By a love
That was cursed.

A grasp I won't feel again.
I remember that feeling
Of the gaze of her eyes
As we intertwined in the sheets.
She is a grasp I won't ever have again.
I won't ever have her—
Bad days because I can't listen anymore,
Nor her good days.
Cannot listen to her laugh until she snorts again.
How she comforts her surroundings.
They do not understand her means,
How they are displayed in her eyes,
Latching onto the next insignificant other,
Battling any contender for an actual lover.
Such a venomous sage,
She is burning throughout her bedroom
To lure the next one in.

Lost in these emotions,

Under these spells

As if I've been drinking potions.

Changes as the seasons do.
Dear, you are beautiful
In and out,
No matter the color of your hair.
Leave the doubt,
For he is not worth the pain you bear.
She says to me,
"How dare?
Dare to reason without my apologies,
To look past my flaws,
To see the fallacy?"

She's asking for a round of applause
For all the issues he caused.

We adore feeling empty,
Not very respectfully,
In hopes that
Their soul is as pure as we read it to be.
We believe that there aren't anymore
Broken heart remedies
Left for us to use,
Thinking we are immune to the abuse.
Dear,
There is no need to tie the noose.

V

SEICHE

—Temporary disturbance

The happiness pours
Through her smile.
I stay a while,
An unusual connection.
I don't question my reflection.
She fills my needs,
Presents my unsaid deeds
As a book read out loud.
The feelings spread
Within and without,
Not a sight of doubt.
Don't let go.
Keep my soul.

Perilous dreams
Lost in your mind,
Hard to find.
Are we alive?
Are we passing time?
The days scroll by
As we wonder why
It's not as it seems.

I was in bed with a murderer.
Not the average kind—
This one is after your heart.
She reaches in and out,
Depleting you of all feeling.
What's to become?
A disconnected bond
Scratches along your spine,
Piercing every inch of time.
After,
You will only rewind.
In times of new lovers,
They will never
Overcome her.
As she's brought your mind to death,
Dangling what is left of your heart
In the eyes
For the next soul
She will inhale.

A melancholy fool
Quick to pull a stool
To sit and wonder
How you got here.
Which way to steer?
The objects are said to be
Closer than they appear.
They're nowhere near,
Comfortably empty, emptied of fear.

Waves of emotions,
Lilac skies of broken hearts,
Gradually done with being discreet
To us, every chamber of our hearts.

That releases all fear
We have never understood
From nightmares.
Everything becomes rough.

Trudge through the worst weather.
It changed us.

Crashing through boulders,
All ounces of purity
Through our hearts.

Afloat with comfort and willfulness,
Without a wonder of the difference,
Listening to every step, every sound.

Everything has become hollow.

Vulnerable heart,
Struggle of love and anger,
Only in dreams could they appear.

In the moment
The seasons have changed.

They unraveled every inch
As we intertwined in the sheets.

Lost in these emotions,
In and out.

Thinking we are immune to the abuse
As a book read out loud,
The days scroll by.

In times of new lovers,

Comfortably empty, emptied of fear.

CPSIA information can be obtained
at www.ICGtesting.com
Printed in the USA
LVHW040855241120
672561LV00001B/67